Stop! Stop!

Before you use thi
the grace

Lord Jesus, give m
will really bless me ;

G000015988

Give me the grace
answered again and

Give me the grace to ⌐⌐⌐⌐⌐⌐ that You will become
my very best Friend.

Contents

The **drawings** are by Sara Ann Quirke, Gurteenminogue Murrintown, Co. Wexford. The **cover photo** is taken from a picture of the Merciful Jesus as revealed to Sr. Faustina.

How To Use This Booklet

The first page of each theme contains a **Reflection**. The second page of each contains **Steps in Prayer**. When continuing to use this booklet for daily prayer, you can often skip the reflections, and focus on the steps in prayer. **Where it is suggested that you write your intentions, it is most important that you do so.**

A Wonderful Free Gift

The first time I experienced the real touch of the Lord in my life was when I read that I didn't have to win my salvation or to work it out by my own efforts. I had tried real hard to do that, but I had failed miserably. Even trying was in itself a pressure, a sort of burden.

I still remember the evening when I read that all I had to do was accept the wonderful gift that Jesus had won for me.

The words just lit up in the middle of a passage. As I read them, a burden fell from my shoulders and I experienced a new sense of freedom.

Yes Jesus has won for you the right to be saved, plus the right to countless other blessings. You don't have to earn them. All that is required of you is to accept them, and to learn how to grow in your openness to them.

Becoming open to them will, of course, have a major impact on your life. A man floundering in a bog hole can't agree to be lifted out of the bog hole and yet still decide to stay in it. He has to choose which he really wants.

If you desire to be saved from the spiritual and moral bog hole, the good news is that Jesus has already won for you the right to be lifted out. All you have to do is to accept your salvation as a free gift, and then seek to become more and more open to that free gift by the way in which you live.

Not merely has Jesus won for you the right to be saved, but also the right to receive countless blessings that will help you in your daily life. He desires to give you all the strength you need to live a happy, fulfilled, transformed life.

Accept the free gift

Steps In Prayer

Lord Jesus, thank You for winning for me the right to eternal life, and the right to have a happy, fulfilled life.

(Pause to take in what you have prayed)

Lord Jesus, I accept You as my Lord and Saviour, and desire to become open to all the blessings.

(Pause to take in what you have prayed.)

Please inspire me to take the right steps so that I may become open to all that You desire for me.

(Pause to take in what you have prayed.)

The Answer To Emptiness

Things went badly for me in Secondary School. I suffered from a teacher. I suffered at the hands of bullies. It had a devastating effect on my life, took away my self-esteem and my self-confidence, and left me feeling deeply isolated and lonely.

This inner emptiness continued in Seminary. The inner emptiness was like a bottomless pit deep within my chest, like an inner vacuum sucking me in. It also left me with strong suicidal tendencies.

Eventually it even affected my faith. I had tried praying. I had gone to daily Mass. I found myself asking, "If Jesus really is the Bread of Life like He says He is, then why am I feeling so empty?"

Then I read, in 'The Cross and the Switchblade' by David Wilkerson, of troubled people whose lives were being transformed by the power of the Holy Spirit, and I received the faith to believe that that could happen for me also.

Then after I was prayed with, I had an experience of a ball of heat rising in my chest where previously I had experienced the inner emptiness. It kept rising and swirling until it filled my inner being. I just knew that I was being touched by Jesus.

Since then Jesus has been a living presence in my life. He has truly become my best Friend. I know His presence every moment of every day. How He enters your life may differ from the way He entered mine, but He desires to be your best Friend also. He and He alone can take away the inner emptiness and the inner pain. Seek Him until He comes powerfully into your life.

Jesus, my best Friend

Steps In Prayer

Lord Jesus, I desire to have You as my best Friend.
(Pause to take in what you have prayed.)

I desire a living relationship with You.
(Pause to take in what you have prayed.)

I desire for You to become the Bread of Life for me.
(Pause to take in what you have prayed.)

Give me the faith to believe that it is possible, and the faith to persevere until You truly become my best Friend.
(Pause to take in what you have prayed.)

Facing Our Helplessness

The biggest block preventing most people from experiencing the power of God is that they don't realise how much they need it. They don't recognise their need for a power greater than themselves. They think that they are managing fine on their own

Yet each of us have weaknesses. The fact that one's weaknesses are not highly destructive ones, does not mean that they do not exist. They do - and if we cannot identify them, that is even worse!

It is actually a liberating experience to say, "I have a weakness and of my own power I cannot overcome it." When we honestly say that, then we are open to receiving help from the Higher Power.

It is no accident that the very first step in Alcoholics Anonymous and a dozen other similar programmes is, "**We admitted we were powerless over .....**"

Once we admit that we are powerless, then the power of God can flow in. Our admission that we are powerless becomes the window through which the power of God can light up our lives.

As well as moral weaknesses, there are also the situations in which we are nervous or afraid or lacking in confidence. These too can become opportunities to become open to the Higher Power - which is Jesus Himself.

Very Important

Make an honest inventory of your weaknesses. Write a word on the side of the page to represent each one. Your spiritual growth will be in proportion to your acceptance of your weaknesses.

**Recognise that you
have weaknesses
and that you need
the Higher Power**

Steps In Prayer

Become conscious of your weaknesses. (Write them down on side of page - one word will do for each.)

Accept that you are powerless to remove them. Then, with expectant faith, ask Jesus to assist you.

Lord Jesus I humbly accept my weaknesses and that I am powerless to remove them.
(Pause to realise the meaning of what you have prayed.)

Lord, please teach me how to depend upon Your Higher Power.

Then think of your greatest weakness and mentally picture yourself being lifted up by power from on high.

Thank you Jesus, that in my weakness, You will lift me up and set me free.

Receiving The Power (1)

"You shall receive power when the Holy Spirit has come upon you." Acts 1: 8

Mel had sunk to the depths of degradation through alcoholism. Given money to run to the chemist for medicine that was urgently needed to save his little girl's life, he ran instead to the pub. When he came home that night, he took the shoes off her dead body and sold them for more drink. But Mel was to have his life transformed by a Power greater than his addiction. The Alcoholics Anonymous movement specialises in helping people to become open to that power, the Higher Power as they call it.

But this Higher Power is there for everybody and not just alcoholics.

St. Paul tells us that it is the same mighty power by which the Father raised Jesus from the dead. He prays that the eyes of our minds may be opened so that we may recognise how "infinitely great" this power is (Eph. 1: 19).

The Greek word here for power is DUNAMIS, the word from which we get the word dynamite. There is a dynamic power that can transform lives; a dynamic power that can enable us to rise above our inhibitions, our shyness and our nervousness; a dynamic power that can enable us to reach our God given potential; a dynamic power that could enable us to do what otherwise would be impossible.

The challenge is to become open to it, to find a way of learning to rely on it. The first step is to recognise that in certain areas of our lives we are powerless. The second step is to focus on becoming open to this power from on high and to learn how to depend upon it.

Steps In Prayer

Write down your weaknesses - one word will do.

Lord I accept that I am powerless over .....   Teach me Lord how to become open to Your power .

Become conscious also of situations in which you find it hard to cope or are nervous. Write them down also - a word will do.

Lord I find it hard to cope when .....   Lift me up, Lord. Enable me to deal with it.

(Mentally picture Jesus doing just that for you.)

Lord give me the faith to believe that by learning to depend on Your power, I can experience a whole new quality of life.

(Pause to take in the meaning of what you have prayed.)

Receiving The Power (2)

"Glory be to God who by this mighty power at work within us is able to do far more then we would ever dare to ask for or dream of." (Eph. 3: 20 TLB)

Mary had been failing her driving test for years, and had spent all her money on lessons. It wasn't that she couldn't drive but rather that her nervousness during the test caused her to make mistakes. She came to me for a blessing. Instead I did a session with her on learning how to depend on the Higher Power. She really gave it a try - and, as a result, passed her test with flying colours.

The method I taught Mary is a method I have used millions of times myself.

First allow into one's mind a vague mental picture of Jesus. It is best if it is not a clear image - then one doesn't get distracted with the details.

Next practise holding that image in your mind even as you walk and talk. See strength coming to you from Jesus, power from on high that will enable you to do what would otherwise be beyond you.

In my early years as a priest, I was petrified when speaking in public. But I succeeded because even as I preached, in the top of my mind, I was clinging to and drawing strength from this image of Jesus. It will work for you too - if you give it a real chance.

This is not make-belief. **Jesus really IS with you, and He delights in giving you this strengthening power**. All you are doing is opening the eyes of your mind to what really is there for you - just as St. Paul prayed that the eyes of our mind would be opened to see this power.

Learn to draw strength from Me

Steps In Prayer

Mentally picture Jesus just above and in front of you. Then "see" power and strength coming from Jesus to set you free from your compulsions and addictions. (Continue to hold this image in your mind for a moment.)

Then "see" yourself being able to walk into difficult situations drawing all the strength you need from Jesus. (Continue to hold this image in your mind for a moment.)

Lord Jesus, I believe in your power to transform my life. I believe that by learning to depend on You, I can do what would otherwise be impossible for me.

Mentally picture yourself being lifted up by Jesus, and gliding through what you find difficult.

Receiving The Power (3)

Remember again that the very same Higher Power that enables chronic alcoholics to break their drink problem and to rebuild their lives is there for you too. It doesn't matter what the addiction or the compulsion is, by learning to depend on this Higher Power, you too can be set free.

Equally, by learning how to draw strength from this Higher Power, you can receive strength for daily living, and the ability to cope in stressful situations.

Even in non-stressful situations, by learning to rely on this Higher Power, you can achieve more than if you rely solely on your own strength.

When the Holy Spirit came upon the Apostles, they were hiding in the upper room for fear of the Jews. After the Holy Spirit came, they went out and preached boldly without fear of anyone.

Naturally for one to become truly open to the Higher Power, it is important to desire to be free of ongoing sin. If there is an area of ongoing sin in your life, let that be the first area in which you accept that you are powerless and that you seek the Higher Power.

The second image I suggest for learning to rely on the Higher Power, is the image of a mighty waterfall. Imagine that the water is warm, and picture yourself being refreshed as it falls upon you.

Then instead of water, **visualise a mighty stream of strengthening power flowing down from heaven**. Desire for it to flood your life. Picture yourself being refreshed, renewed and cleansed by it. This image too can become a mighty channel of God's anointing.

Steps In Prayer
"You shall receive power when the Holy Spirit has come upon you." Acts 1: 8

Pause to really desire this power to touch your life.

Then form a mental image of a great 'waterfall' of power flowing down from heaven, and of yourself being refreshed, cleansed and renewed by this outpouring.

O Holy Spirit come upon me as You came upon the Apostles at Pentecost. Flood me with this power from on high so that I may be cleansed and renewed.
(Pause to take in what you have prayed.)

Dear Lord, I'm Desperate

It was October, 2001. Joanne, my wonderful secretary of 13 years was leaving. The Christmas rush was coming - and so too was the extra work arising from the Euro change-over. With the two of us working flat out, it would have been extremely challenging, but for myself on my own, it would have been utterly impossible. I found myself crying out again and again, **"Lord, I'm desperate."**

It is amazing how one can become open to new possibilities at a time like that. One is forced to surrender everything to God, and sometimes, if we listen, He can reveal something extra of His plan for us; something that we would have completely missed had everything run smoothly.

After a couple of panic filled days it struck me that, rather than taking on one person full time, I should take on three or four people part-time.

Where the Lord is leading me today has moved on from where He led me when I first took on a full time secretary many years ago. Had the rug not been pulled from under my feet, I would have missed this new leading entirely.

So too Jesus can use the upsets and crises in your life, to lead you into new openings. Turn to Him now with whatever difficulty you face, expecting Him to bring good out of it for you.

Faith becomes real faith when we learn to trust Jesus even when we face desperate situations. In the crisis situations, learn to trust that Jesus has a special plan for your life, and that there will be a way forward. First express how you really feel, then surrender the entire situation to Jesus, then start trusting the He will bring you through.

Bring
your problems
to Me

Steps In Prayer

Lord Jesus, I really am desperate. I cry out to You for help. Help me to cope with this situation, and to make the right decisions.

(Pause to hold your prayer before Jesus.)

Lord, I believe the Bible promise that You work all things for the good for those who love You. Lord in faith, I trust that You are somehow going to bring good out of this situation. Lord, in faith, I believe that You will lead me into Your special plan for my life.

(Pause to take in what you have prayed)

17

Desire Answer To Prayer?

God loves You. He desires to bless you. Just as a normal father or mother desires what is good for their children, so too God desires what is best for you. But He needs your cooperation to help bring about His special plan for you and the blessings He desires to give you.

Few of us become open to even 75% of the blessings that God desires to give us. The vast majority don't even begin to realise how much they are missing out on.

Of course, there are some requests He won't answer - what mother will give her child a bar of chocolate half an hour before dinner! I often thank God that some of my petitions were not granted, for with hindsight I can see that He had something better for me.

But meanwhile there are so many blessings that He does desire to grant you. Becoming open to them requires repentance of sin, an expectant faith, and a desire to come into God's plan for your life. Add in bringing your intentions before Jesus through prayer.

Very important
On the margins of the next page write down your intentions, one word for each will do.

Writing down your intentions helps to make them concrete. They are no longer just a thought (or a worry) floating in the back of your mind. And when you come back to this page, they are there before you immediately, reminding you to again bring them before Jesus in expectant prayer.

Pray like this on a daily basis, and you will see many prayers answered.

Steps In Prayer
"Whatsoever you ask in prayer, believe that you receive it, and you will" Mark 11:24 (RSV).
(Pause to take in the meaning of this promise.)

Select one of the intentions you have written down, hold it before Jesus, and mentally picture Jesus bringing blessing into the situation.

Then pray three times, continuing to 'see' blessing flowing from Jesus into the situation as you pray,
May Your Sacred Heart, Lord Jesus, be praised, glorified and honoured throughout the whole world now and for ever more.

Then select a second intention and repeat the process, and perhaps the same with a third.

Learn to pray like this whenever a need arises even in the middle of your work and daily life.

Coping With Misfortune

Bad things happen to good people. Things will go wrong on you. Sometimes they will go very wrong - accidents, sickness, misfortunes, etc.

Sometimes too all hell may appear to break loose in one's personal relationships. People will betray you, let you down, turn against you.

Sometimes it may be your own mistakes or even sin that brings the ceiling tumbling down upon you. Other times you may be completely blameless.

The good news is that regardless of how the problem has come about, Jesus desires to give you all the strength that you need.

If He does not remove the bad thing, He is more than willing to make you a hero in the way you cope with it. Make a decision that you are going to place the whole situation in His hands, seek to do things His way, and rely on His power, then trust that He will bring you through the crisis and, in some way, bring good out of it for you.

The Bible promises, "Commit your cause to the Lord and He will act on your behalf" Ps. 37:5.

I am not saying that it will be easy. I am not saying that you won't have to suffer. But what I do guarantee is that if you really hand the situation over to Jesus, seek to do things His way, and learn to rely on His power, that He will bring you through - and bring blessing out of the situation for you.

I speak from experience! What He has done for me, He desires to do for you too.

Steps in Prayer

Become conscious of the trials or challenges you face.

Write down one word to represent each trial or challenge.

Lord Jesus, I bring this trial to You. Help me to place it fully in Your hands, (pause), and to leave it there.
(Pause to picture yourself doing that.)

Help me to respond to this situation your way.
(Again pause to picture yourself doing that.)

Lord I am helpless over this situation. Help me to rely on Your power and to draw my strength from You.
(Again pause to picture yourself doing that.)

Growing In The Blessing

Some time ago, I had a dream in which I reminded Bishop Comiskey of how on the Jubilee of his ordination, he spoke very humbly and honestly to us priests about the struggle he had to give up drink; how at the treatment centre, he had tried everything, but it was only when the programme and everything else had failed, and he had come before God totally helpless, that he was delivered.

In my dream I said to him, "What a pity you haven't shared that story more widely. Now you must go back to that experience, re-root your whole life in it and make it the centre of your ministry."

Later I realised that there was a message in the dream that applied to myself, and indeed to everyone:- **Get in touch with the moment or moments when God touched your life.** Call those moments to mind, seek to re-root your whole life in them, and to make them the centre of your plans.

St. Paul said something similar to Timothy, "Fan into flames the spiritual gift God gave you" 2 Tm. 1: 6 TLB

The fundamental spiritual gift is the experience of being touched by God's love. We need to draw both our inspiration and our sense of direction from those special moments. By recalling them, we will help to "fan into flames the spiritual gift" that God gave us.

Its impact on our lives will then grow until it truly becomes a transforming power at the very centre of our being. So think back to the times you experienced a sense of being touched or blessed by God, and allow yourself to relive the experience.

If the gift appears small,
remember that great oaks
from tiny acorns grow.

Steps in Prayer

Become conscious of moments when you felt the closeness of God, or a sense of being blessed by Him. Allow yourself to re-experience what it was like. (Pause.)

Become conscious that Jesus desires for this moment of blessing to become for you an ongoing experience; and that He desires for you to be filled with a sense of His love. (Pause to mentally picture this happening.)

Lord Jesus, thank You for the moments when You touched my life. Help me to re-root my whole life in them and help me to build my life upon them.
(Pause to take in what you have prayed.)

See The Bigger Picture

Very few of us set out to bring hurt or disappointment into the lives of others, yet often we end up doing so. We can greatly reduce the danger of that happening by doing regular checks on our priorities and our lifestyle.

Sometimes something really annoys us and we end up lashing out in a destructive way.

Sometimes hurt or dislike builds up, and we fail to deal with it - even though it may lead to disastrous divisions in the home or the community.

Sometimes we give into temptation without thinking of the consequences. It could be sexual temptation, or the abuse of alcohol, or it could involve dishonesty.

Sometimes we can become so caught up in what we are doing that we neglect something or someone else.

Sometimes we may follow whatever appears most exciting, and neglect what we should be doing.

Sometimes we may allow inappropriate friendships to develop or good friendships to develop in an inappropriate way.

To help us avoid these pitfalls, we need some image of what we desire to be and to achieve in life .

This image and sense of direction will help to keep us from wrong choices, and when we do make wrong choices, it will help us to spot the mistake, and to turn back.

Very Important
At least once a month, go through the above checklist.

Whatever the issue, be reconciled

Steps In Prayer

Lord Jesus I repent of every time that I have brought hurt or disappointment into the lives of others, and I desire where possible to make reparation.

(Pause to allow the Holy Spirit to prompt you.)

Lord, if there is something in the way I am currently living that could cause hurt to others, help me to see it and to deal with it.

(Pause to allow the Holy Spirit to prompt you.)

Lord, help me to always see the bigger picture, and to think of what is best for my family and my community.

(Pause to allow the Holy Spirit to prompt you.)

At least once a month, reread the checklist on the previous page

Healing Through Forgiving

When I was ordained, Jesus had already come powerfully into my life, yet I was still full of anger towards those who had brought hurt into my life - and I didn't even see the importance of dealing with my anger.

This anger did not block my having a vital relationship with Jesus, but it did block my spiritual growth, it was damaging me emotionally, and it was spilling over into my relationships and into my handling of conflict situations.

Before I could really grow spiritually and emotionally, I had to face my anger and work towards forgiveness. How I now wish that I had done that far sooner.

I can now see that until I forgave, my inner anger was leading me to hurt others, and also that inner healing and spiritual growth speeded up immensely after I forgave.

As well as the hurts from the past, there are the things that create anger within us now. Some have to live in very stressful or unfair situations, while sometimes we may even be angry about issues far removed from ourselves.

Whatever the source of our anger, it is very important that we acknowledge it, and get in touch with it. Sometimes anger can be a positive thing - it causes us to stand for issues and to challenge wrongdoing. But it is important to honestly acknowledge your anger. Acknowledge it to yourself, to God, and, if it is ongoing, to a trustworthy friend.

Most often our anger, having been acknowledged, needs to be challenged and dealt with. If we really desire to come into healing and to mature, we need to work through our anger and to learn forgiveness - especially for what has happened in the past.

Let the light shine into your heart

Steps In Prayer

Become conscious of anything that is making you angry. Acknowledge your anger and bring it before God.

Lord this really does make me angry. It really ......

Lord, with Your help I can handle this anger in an appropriate way.

Pause to picture yourself drawing strength from Jesus.

Lord Jesus, on the cross You prayed, "Father forgive them for they know not what they do." When I find it hard to forgive, help me to pray like that. Help me to take the steps necessary to come into forgiveness

(Pause to take in what you have prayed)

Finding God's Special Plan

It was about a year before my ordination. There was a strong chance that after ordination, I would be asked to teach and the idea didn't appeal to me at all. If I wasn't teaching, I was likely to be sent abroad, and I didn't really fancy that either. So over a period, I was asking the Lord for guidance.

One day I glanced at a magazine and a quotation from Acts absolutely lit up, **"We will devote ourselves to prayer and to preaching"**. Back then I was a hopeless speaker and crippled with shyness into the bargain, but I knew then that this was what Jesus was calling me to do.

I got accepted into the Mission House but after just three years, I was sent to do parish work. I spent 25 years in parish work, yet I always knew that my real calling was to "prayer and preaching", or as the sentence in Acts is more correctly translated, "prayer and the ministry of the word". Gradually my writing ministry built up, and I am now leaving parish work to pray, write and preach.

Jesus has a special plan for you too. For some this will involve big decisions. For others it involves becoming the best that one can be in the context of the decisions that one has already made; becoming the best husband or wife, father or mother, priest or sister or dedicated single person that one can be, together with developing one's work or business to its maximum.

Not merely has God a special plan for our lives, but He delights in helping us to find it - so go on asking Him to show you the way forward. Ask Him to give you a vision of where He is leading you in life, of His overall plan for you.

Steps In Prayer

"If you want to know what God wants you to do, ask Him, and He will delight in showing you the way."
James 1:5 (paraphrased).
Pause a moment to breathe in those words.

Become conscious that Jesus really does have a plan for your life, and that His plan is to bless.

Lord Jesus, I really do desire to become open to your plan for my life.
Pause to take in what you have prayed

Please help me to make the right choices, and if I am ever stepping outside Your plan for my life, please block me.

Renounce Worrying

Worrying has never solved any problem - all it does is sap one's energy. Indeed it often takes away the inner peace that is needed to discern where God is leading.

Dr. Charles Mayo, of the famous Mayo clinic, has said, "There is a growing mountain of evidence to suggest that worry is the chief contributor to depression, nervous breakdowns, high blood pressure, heart attacks, and early death."

Then there is the devastating effect that it has on our spirit, the way it destroys our trust in Jesus. Thus any tendency to worry needs to be challenged and renounced.

For some, worrying has become a compulsive habit. They no longer have control over it. When that happens one must accept that one is powerless over one's tendency to worry. Then turn to Jesus who is the Higher Power.

Make a decision that you are going to rely on His help for this day; that for this day, by His power, you are going to renounce worrying and trust in Him.

Entrust Your whole life to Him, and all that is in it. Then see yourself going through this day drawing strength and power from on high, holding an image of Jesus before your mind.

Very Important

Identify anything that is playing on your mind. Write it on the side of the page - one word will do.

Then make a decision that you are handing this situation over to God. When you come back to the page tomorrow, check how you have been doing.

"See I have carved you on the palms of my hands." Is 49:16

Steps In Prayer

Become conscious of anything that has been playing on your mind. Then take in the words,

"Do not worry about anything ... " **Phil 4:6**

Fear not, for I have redeemed you;
I have called you by name, you are Mine.
When you pass through the waters,
I will be with you, and through the rivers, they
shall not overwhelm you. (Isaiah 43:1-2 RSV)

Mentally picture Jesus bringing you through every crisis.

Lord Jesus, help me to renounce my worrying,
and for this day to trust You for everything and
with everything

Mentally picture that happening.

31

The Power In The Mass

There was a huge throng of people around Jesus, with plenty of hustle and bustle. Suddenly Jesus declared that "power" had gone out from Him. One woman, who had suffered from a haemorrhage for many years and who had spent all her money on doctors, had the faith to believe that if she could just touch the hem of His garment she would be healed.

Hundreds of others had touched Him, but it had done them no good. She alone experienced the power.

The same happens at Mass. In every church there are a small number of people who really believe in what happens during Mass, who really believe that Jesus comes on the altar, who really believe that Jesus comes to them in Holy Communion.

For them every Mass is a wonderful occasion, a treasured experience, a real encounter with Jesus. They experience the power and it brings them joy.

You too can experience the power, but to do so, you must thirst for it.

Decide to accept in faith that Jesus really comes under the form of bread and wine. This is not something you can work out with your mind. But if we believe in Jesus, then we can believe in what He said, and He said, "This is my body."

Then, every time you go to Mass or even think about the Mass, desire to be touched by His power; desire to be drawn into His closeness, to be embraced by His love; desire a fresh outpouring of His blessing, His anointing. Learn to always come to Mass with expectant faith.

Steps In Prayer

Allow yourself to have a sense of longing to really meet Jesus in the Mass, and to be touched by the power emanating from Him.

Lord Jesus, help me to have faith like the faith of the woman who touched the hem of your garment.
(Pause to open your heart in faith to Jesus.)

Help me to really believe that when I receive Holy Communion, I really receive You.
(Pause to open your heart in faith to Jesus.)

Help me to approach every Mass expecting to be touched by power flowing from You.
(Picture yourself being touched by power from on high.)

A Friend In Heaven

On one occasion when Sr. Briege McKenna was praying with me, she received an image of blessings being poured out as I led the saying of the Memorare, (the prayer on the next page). What Sr. Briege could not have known is that I very often include the Memorare during Mass. I find it a powerful prayer.

I find it almost impossible to truly pray the Rosary, that is to keep my mind on it. **But that has not prevented me from having a wonderful relationship with our Blessed Mother.**

So too can you. When we accept Jesus into our lives, He doesn't come alone. In Jesus, we receive a whole new family. The saints and angels become part of our heavenly family. Just as Moses and Elijah visited with Jesus on Mount Tabor, so too Our Lady, and the great saints, can visit with us and be instruments of blessing for us.

As Jesus said, the saints are like unto the angels, and just as the angels can bring us something of God's love and blessing, so too can the great saints.

Being close to Our Lady in no way diminishes your relationship with Jesus - on the contrary, it enhances it; Think of your best friend here on earth. If the situation is normal, getting to know your best friend's family will have enriched your friendship. So too with Jesus' family.

It will help you to grow in your relationship with Our Lady if you learn to form a mental picture of her.

Mentally picture her radiating God's love and blessing to you. When praying for others, picture her standing beside them, imparting to them her motherly blessing.